Shapes

by Tristan Horrom
illustrated by John Hovel

Pre-Decodable 9

McGraw Hill Education

Bothell, WA • Chicago, IL • Columbus, OH • New York, NY

MHEonline.com

Send all inquiries to:
McGraw-Hill Education
8787 Orion Place
Columbus, OH 43240

ISBN: 978-0-02-143411-4
MHID: 0-02-143411-5

Printed in China

9 10 11 12 13 DSS 28 27 26 25 24

I had a  .

square

I had a  .

triangle

I had a  .

rectangle

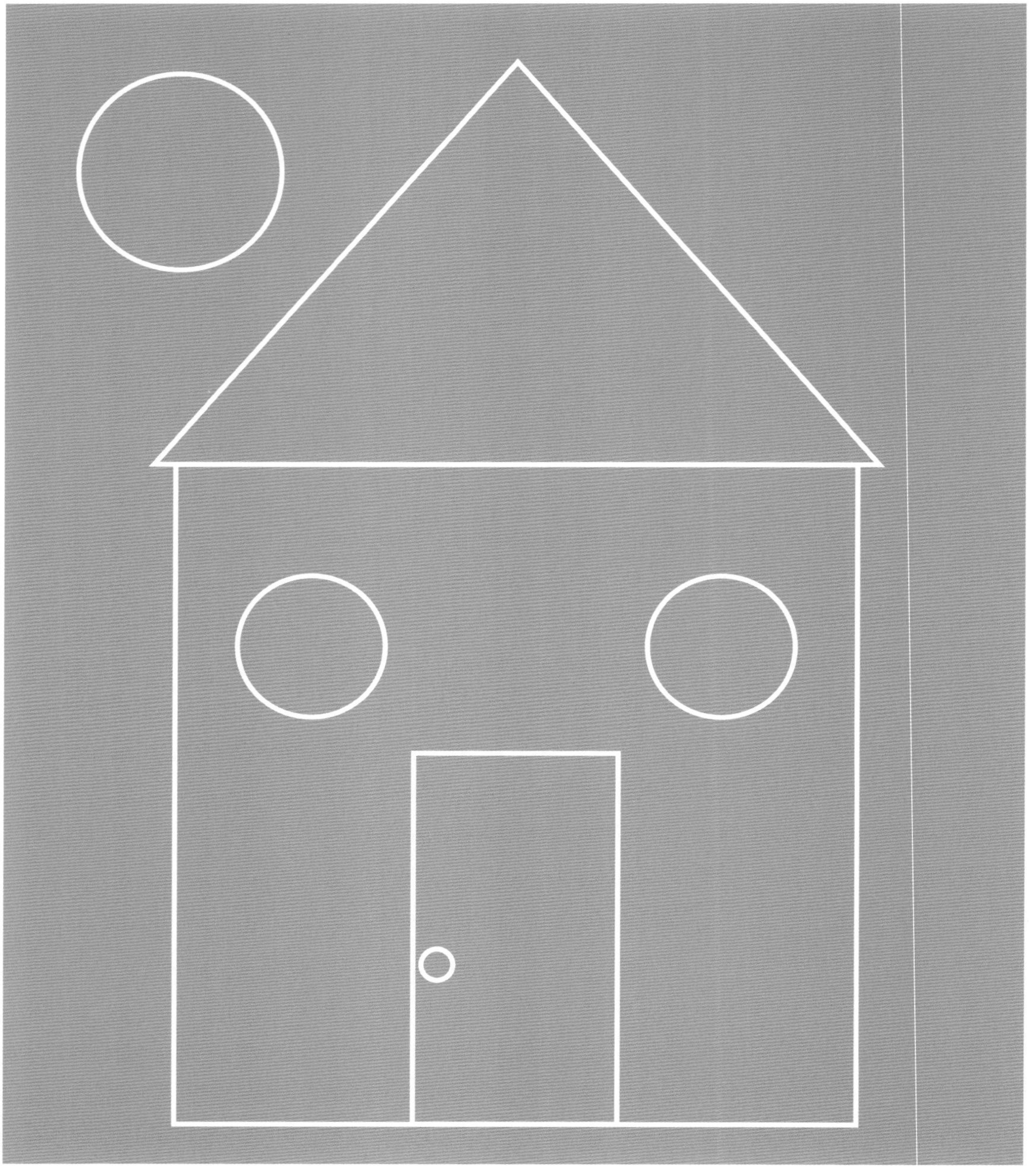

I had 4 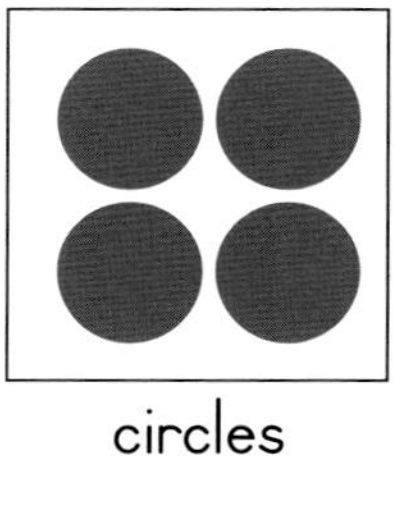 .

four circles

I had 5  .

five stars

I had a  !

house